DENNIS STOCK

Provence Memories

Introduction by
PHILIP CONISBEE

A New York Graphic Society Book
Little, Brown and Company - Boston

Illustration credits:
Vincent Van Gogh, *Olive Trees, 1889.*
Oil on canvas. The William Hood Dunwoody Fund.
Courtesy, The Minneapolis Institute of Arts.

Paul Gauguin, *Les Alyscamps, Arles, 1889.*
Oil on canvas. Courtesy, Musée d'Orsay, Paris.

Paul Cézanne, *Landscape in Provence, c. 1880.*
French, 1839-1906. Oil on canvas.
21 1/2 × 25 3/4 in. (54.5 × 65.5 cm.) 9.1981.
Restricted anonymous loan.
Photo: courtesy, Museum of Fine Arts, Boston.

ISBN 0-8212-1715-1

Library of Congress Catalog Card Number: 88-81007

First U.S. edition

New York Graphic Society books are published by
Little, Brown and Company (Inc.)
Published simultaneously in Canada by
Little, Brown & Company (Canada) Limited

PRINTED IN ITALY

There are many Provences. To the west, it is the land of the grand, broad River Rhône, flowing by picturesque ancient cities such as Avignon, Beaucaire, Tarascon and Arles, and out to the sea through its flat, open, grassy estuary area of the Camargue. To the south, Provence is bounded by the Mediterranean, with one of the busiest and by turns most beautiful coastlines in the world. To the east, towards the border with Italy, it becomes the mountainous land of the Alpes Maritimes; westwards again, there are the craggy Alpilles, or "Little Alps", whose tortured forms engaged Van Gogh; the monumental Mont Sainte-Victoire, celebrated by Cézanne; and the spectacularly scenic Gorges du Verdon. It is the land of awesome Roman remains: the arenas and theatres of Arles and Orange, the ancient burial ground of the Alyscamps, the mausoleum and arches at Les Antiques of Saint-Remy and at Orange, and part of an excavated city at Vaison-la-Romaine. It is also the land of exquisite Romanesque churches, such as Saint-Trophîme at Arles or Saint-Gilles-du-Gard; but also many a less famous small church, its belltower over the red roofs of some little town, awaiting the discovery of the curious traveller. There is the Gothic Palais des Papes in old papal Avignon, with its early Italian fresco decorations, and the elegant 18th-century Archbishop's Palace in Aix-en-Provence, now a museum of tapestries and a beautiful setting for summertime concerts of Mozart. It is a fertile land of vines and twisting olives, honey and almonds, plane trees, pines and cypresses, garlic and nectarines, sunflowers and lavender, and the aromatic bouquet of herbs we know as *herbes de Provence*; seemingly all the fruits of the earth and of the sea too. Wherever one travels, there are the characteristic red-tiled roofs and colorwashed walls in ochre, sienna and umber, of an isolated *mas*, or small farm, and of houses clustered in the dusty towns of the plain, or in the high airy hill towns which sometimes seem to grow out of the rock.

The modern Provençal artistic heritage that we share and enjoy most readily – that of Cézanne and Van Gogh, and the next generation of Braque, Matisse and Picasso – was nurtured by a long cultural tradition. If Hercules did mythic battle with giants on the fertile plain of La Crau, whose stones are there to remind us of his mortal combat; and the Carthaginian Hannibal passed this way from Spain to Italy, of course they left no real trace to compare even with the scant remains of the Phoenecians and the Greeks. However, the Romans are still powerfully present in Provence in their great surviving monuments, but haunted by the spirits of the vanquished Gauls of Entremont, whose noble and moving artistic remains have been uncovered and can be seen in the Musée Granet at Aix-en-Provence. Roman Imperial Arles in turn nurtured a sort of Roman renascence in the 12th century – but at the service of the Christian ethos – in churches such as Saint-Trophîme, making for an indigenous classical tradition. Thus with such a history and in the sharp shadowed southern sun, the classical rhythms of the 17th and 18th-century noble houses and public buildings of Avignon, Aix-en-Provence and Marseilles (as it was before World War II), or of, say, the old Bishop's Palace in a once great town like Carpentras, seem natural here. But it would be stretching a point to seriously suggest that those early stone carvers and classical architects were inspired by the look and feel of the place, by the *genius loci*, by the dense shadow of a pine in summer, or by the high-angled fall of the sun on a craggy rock that they might have passed, like Cézanne after them, on a hot Provençal road. Well, it is at least our late Romantic privilege to speculate thus, as we mingle in our thoughts and reveries, art and nature, memory and desire.

"I must tell you that I am still occupied with my painting and that there are treasures to be taken away from this country, which has not yet found an interpreter equal to the abundance

Olive Trees, 1889, Vincent Van Gogh. Courtesy, The Minneapolis Institute of Arts.

of riches which it displays." Writing from the small hill town of Gardanne in May 1886, Paul Cézanne was effectively announcing what was to be his chief mission as a painter – to be the greatest interpreter of his native Provence. From this year onwards, he more-or-less abandoned the stresses and strains of the Parisian art world, and devoted himself to celebrating the rigors and the beauties of that ancient, sun-drenched landscape, redolent as it was of deep memories of his youth. He did indeed become the most famous painter of Provence and his example encouraged several generations of artists to follow him to the warm South in search of the special inspiration of that magical region. Of course for the modern visitor to Provence – or for the viewer of Dennis Stock's photographs in this volume – some of that magic comes from our association of Provence with the visions it inspired in some of the greatest artists of the modern era.

Cézanne and Van Gogh may have claimed pre-eminence for themselves as the first authentic interpreters of that special region. But their visions, seminal for the modern tradition in art, have stimulated successive generations of painters, draftsmen and photographers too, to seek out the uniquely inspiring qualities of the Provençal landscape. Both masters had a sense that they were at the beginning of something new and we, with our hindsight, can follow the artistic implications of their achievements, subtly intertwined as they are with the inspiration of the place itself, down to our own day and to more modern means of representation. There is indeed a distinctive look and feel to the place – a real *genius loci* – that captures the eye and the heart of anyone who lingers there, and that continues to inspire. Of course any artist, be he or she painter, draftsman or photographer, responds to it both through their own subjectivity and through the particular qualities of their technical means; yet *it* – the look which is the outward man-

ifestation of the spirit of Provence – subtly, deeply, asserts its presence in their work. Typically, the photographs of Dennis Stock embody the ongoing tradition of representing Provence – in some of his chosen themes, for example – but his sensibility, his methods of work as a photographer, his "angle of vision" in every sense of the phrase, and his feeling for the place itself, its special light, colors, textures, are subtly imbued with that spirit. It is for the viewer to contemplate the interweaving of tradition and innovation, perception and invention, nature and photographic art.

For all that Cézanne worked in a relatively restricted area of Provence, around Aix-en-Provence and its immediately neighboring small towns and villages, at the red-earthed Bibémus Quarry, in the foothills of the Mont Sainte-Victoire, and further south to the coast at L'Estaque near Marseilles – he seems to have captured the essence of the whole region. Or perhaps it is rather the case that anyone who has grown to love Cézanne's art will tend to see Provence through his eyes. The peculiar intensity of his vision and the depth of his understanding come from the fact that he saw not with the eyes of the visitor in search of the picturesque, but as an artist who was drawing on rich childhood associations with this very landscape. Here he had passed the happy times of his childhood and youth with the young Emile Zola and other friends, walking, climbing, camping out under the stars, and bathing in rivers and ponds in the shadow of the great Sainte-Victoire. When Zola began to develop his literary career in Paris, he and Cézanne exchanged many a nostalgic letter about their carefree years, "in the country of bouillabaisse and aioli". In a quite Romantic way, Cézanne always insisted on painting out-of-doors, to immerse himself in the total experience of the nature he loved, and the better to *realise* that love, that sensation, in his paintings. In 1898, when Cézanne was at last gaining some

Les Alyscamps, Arles, 1889, Paul Gauguin. Courtesy, Musée d'Orsay, Paris.

reputation with a discriminating public, his friend the Aix-en-Provence poet, critic and editor Joachim Gasquet saw embodied in Cézanne's work the very soul of Provence, in a review of a patriotic book on the medieval history of the region: "The soul, the idea of Provence slumbers under the olive trees, the strong lines of the landscape embrace it, the pine trees give it their perfume, the sun exalts it... and this idea, which is concealed in a thousand places, scattered and blurred, in the red earth, the rocks, the radiant pine trees, the planes and hills – one day, when I looked at Cézanne's landscape, I suddenly saw it spring up in its strong synthesis, in its unique splendor, both rural and mystical; it dominates in magnificent reality the whole work of this master."

Cézanne was not the first painter to celebrate that independent, vibrant landscape, nor the first to go out and "realise his sensations" by painting out-of-doors before the *motif*. Since the late 18th century, when nature and landscape became such important preoccupations of early Romantic artists, there had been a vigorous local tradition of landscape painting. The founder of this school had been Jean-Antoine Constantin (1756-1844), who studied at the Marseilles Academy and in Rome, and came to Aix-en-Provence in 1786 as professor of the small art academy there. Constantin drew and painted historicised landscapes in the classical manner, and also views of the area between Aix-en-Provence and Marseilles. He made some vivid and free oil sketches in the open air, and passed on this direct approach to nature to his pupil François-Marius Granet (1775-1849). The Musée Granet in Aix-en-Provence has quantities of nature drawings and oil sketches by Constantin and by Granet, including some by the younger painter of the Mont Sainte-Victoire. A later generation of landscape painters, such as Prosper Grésy (1804-1874) and Emile Loubon (1809-1863), moved away from classical conventions, and came to terms

during the 1840s with the radical Realism of Gustave Courbet in Paris and the Barbizon painters. They and younger painters, in the 1850s and 1860s, such as Marius Engalière (1824-1857) and Paul Guigou (1834-1871) turned their attention more-or-less constantly to the depiction of the Provençal scene, its pastoral life, and its distinctive, tough, often rocky and inhospitable landscape, including the dominant masses of the Mont Sainte-Victoire. Their intense pictorial interest in their native land paralleled the literary concerns of the writers of the contemporary Félibrige movement of the 1850s, to which we return below.

It was in large part the example of Cézanne, however, that encouraged Vincent Van Gogh to sequester himself in Provence in 1888 – but further west, in and around Arles and Saint-Rémy. Gauguin, another founder of modern art in search of the primitive, was to join Van Gogh in Arles for a brief and stormy period, and was also inspired by the spirit of the place. No less than Cézanne, Van Gogh imposed his own intense vision on the landscape of Provence, causing the olives and the cypresses to twist and undulate, the skies and cornfields to swirl, in expression both of his own joy in nature and the anguish in his heart. *"Nature and fine weather,"* he wrote, "are the advantages of the South." Several times he spoke of his desire to make paintings "of the South," and once he conceived of the totality of his Provençal paintings as "at best a sort of whole, *Impressions of Provence.*" He found inspiration not only in the work of other admired artists, such as Cézanne, but also in the color and light of Provence, "the land of the blue tones and gay colors," above all in the characteristic heat of summer, where he saw "old gold, bronze, copper one might say, with the green azure of the sky blenched with heat: a delicious color, extraordinarily harmonious, with the blended tones of Delacroix."

Difficult as it was for Van Gogh to find models to sit for him,

Landscape in Provence, c. 1880, Paul Cézanne. Photo, courtesy, Museum of Fine Arts, Boston.

he more than Cézanne had a powerful sense of the working harmony of man and nature in Provence. He made moving images of the labors of the fields, inspired by the sober peasant scenes of Jean-François Millet, with ploughmen and sowers working their rich soil, while others tend their vines. Van Gogh had also set off to Provence in search of a sort of primitivism; he compared Provence to Japan, or the pretty gipsy girls of Les Saintes-Maries-de-la-Mer to the statuesque figures of Cimabue and Giotto.

Indeed, historically there had always been something primitive, authentic and "apart" about Provence, far as it was from the center of administrative power in Paris. Variously pulled throughout its history, now towards France, now towards Savoy, now towards Italy, only in the Revolutionary year of 1791 was Provence finally assimilated to France. Further attempts to end the relative cultural, political and economic independence of Provence were made after the accession of Emperor Napoleon III in 1851, for example in making the teaching of the French language compulsory in schools. Along with the musical southern version of French, the vernacular language of many people was Provençal – as it still is in some rural communities – a locally named version of the ancient Langue d'Oc, the old language of southern France from the Atlantic to Italy. Attempts at metropolitan French cultural domination sharpened the awareness of Provençal intellectuals, artists and writers, and stimulated a vigorous reassertion of their traditional culture. This was led by the writer and poet Frédéric Mistral (1830-1914), who with other Provençal writers such as Joseph Roumanille (1818-1891) and Théodore Aubanel (1829-1886) met in 1854 at the Château de Font-Ségugne near Avignon and founded a society called the Félibrige, devoted to the study and promotion of the Provençal language and other threatened aspects of local culture. They published journals in the Provençal language, Mistral compiled a great Provençal dictionary, *Trésor du Félibrige*, and wrote books, plays and poems in Provençal. He was also active in founding the Museon Arlaten in Arles, devoted to the presentation of local popular and artistic culture, lore and customs. It is from this period that dates the notion of the special beauty of the Arlesienne, in her traditional costume and jewelry, and who is extolled in all the 19th-century guidebooks to Provence. Van Gogh complained that none would sit for him.

The Félibres, as the group called themselves (and, incidentally, with whom Van Gogh wished to be identified, in a letter of 1888), were extremely important not only in Provence, where they stimulated pride in local culture, but elsewhere in France and Europe, where regionalism was developing as an authentic cultural resistance to the encroachments of an increasingly centralised and uniform modern industrial and economic world. The high moment of Provence's literary tradition had been in the Middle Ages, with its greatest contribution to European literature being the lyric poetry of the Troubadours (itself a Provençal word meaning composer or poet), in the 12th century especially. The songs of the Troubadours were short but very elaborate, and mainly devoted to themes of love, courtship and the cult of women. Romantic poets of the 19th century rediscovered the Troubadours, their work was particularly closely studied by the Félibres, and they have continued to inspire 20th-century poets such as Ezra Pound. An intense local pride in Provence is also found in the work of more popular writers, who by continuing to write in French could reach a wider audience. The most famous of these, who was a younger contemporary of the Félibres but not part of their group, was Alphonse Daudet (1840-97). This tender and sentimental novelist was born in Nîmes, and is best remembered for his humorous sketches of Provençal life collected together in 1868 as *Lettres de Mon Moulin*, referring to the mill where he lived at Font-vieille, near Arles. Among many other works on Provençal themes he also wrote the play *L'Arlésienne* in 1872, with incidental music contributed by Bizet. The popular tradition was continued by Jean Giono (1895-1970) from Monosque, who celebrated in his novels the primitive and down-to-earth rustic life of the region, sensitive to both the beauties and the hardships of a life close to nature. Of exactly the same generation was Marcel Pagnol (1895-1974) from Aubagne, a writer of novels, sometimes bitter and sometimes comic, about life in rural Provence and in the city of Marseilles. Most of the artists and writers discussed above lived and worked in the interior areas of Provence, and took as their raw material its life and landscapes. Dennis Stock's photographs have been made mainly in the Vaucluse, Lubéron, Arles and down to the Camargue. Indeed, only on the Camargue and at the picturesque little town of Les Sainte-Maries-de-la-Mer do we get a hint of the Provençal coast.

But it is that western inland region above all that constitutes the "real" Provence for those who know. The charmed circle is from Marseilles to Arles, to Avignon, to the Mont Ventoux, to Forcalquier, to Manosque and down to the Mont Sainte-Victoire and Aix-en-Provence. It is a place of blazing red soils and bounded by grey, craggy cliffs. And where there is soil, it is worked by a people with gnarled hands that Van Gogh would still recognize; and Cézanne would still find his remote, high hillside tracks, or a secret overgrown quarry, where the only company is the deafening chatter of a million cigales. "I have nothing to complain about," he wrote in May 1886 from Gardanne, "always the sky, the boundless things of nature, attract me and give me the chance to look with pleasure." The distinctive forms and colors of the Provençal sky and landscape, the proud isolation and a local way of life, continue to exert their subtle, inexplicable spell on artists working in all media down to our own day.

Philip Conisbee
Boston, Massachusetts
April, 1988

As a color essayist I am always looking for themes that have considerable potential for pure graphics and suit my sensibility. Southern France filled this need. In Provence large yellow wheat fields dotted with wild red poppies move in unison to the heavy breathing of a "mistral" wind. Isolated farmhouses stand, their worn surfaces covered with patched stonework that testify to their being born from the land and ready to return. The bare limbs of the venerable trees are pruned to their knuckles, often resembling agonized, arthritic hands reaching for the warmth of the southern sun. Rows of lavender carpet and perfume the hillsides. Everywhere working peasants alternate between sowing seeds and gossip. In all seasons this harmonious pastoral paradise stirs the creative soul.

It is a little over a hundred years since Van Gogh stepped off the train in Arles. After that major event writers, poets, painters, and musicians followed, seeking the inspirational sustenance provided by the beauty of Provence. In this century photographers joined the pilgrimage. My exploration started in 1976. For two summers I conducted color workshops at the Festival d'Arles. The Van Gogh imagery was everywhere and our classes constantly sensed his vision in the town and outlying countryside. I photographed very little during that period but my fascination for the area kept growing, and finally in the spring of 1978 I based myself in this environment so rich with light, shapes, texture, colors, and very sympathetic people. Two books have materialized from that seven year period – "Flower Show," which was partially done in Provence and this book, "Provence Memories." I mostly explored the Vaucluse and Bouche de Rhone regions as my home was in the Luberon, a chain of mountains that extend east to west through the heart of the farmlands. Hillside villages and patchwork quilt fields of various crops surrounded me. Many mornings I would load up the car with cameras, tripod, sandwiches, wine, and fruit and set out. The narrow country roads led me into photographic opportunities and encounters that have enriched my life considerably. Farmers tolerated my trespassing and often encouraged forays onto their lands. We all shared in the love of Provence. The new friendships with locals who sympathized with my quest made the creative commitment stronger. Usually, all my concentration is in the making of pictures, but this Mediterranean atmosphere forced me into a more leisurely approach. Here, there is time for everything. Only the seasons set the pace. Urban rhythms have little importance here. Life evolves organically like the crops.

Moving on has not been easy. Provence is a state of mind, with a tangible evidence of perfection. This balanced atmosphere that I often miss was very well observed by Colette in "Belles Saisons I" ... "there is a merciful negligence which gives it an impromptu charm in which the temorary and the permanent collaborate, plantlife and grey stone patched with dusty pink plaster."

Dennis Stock

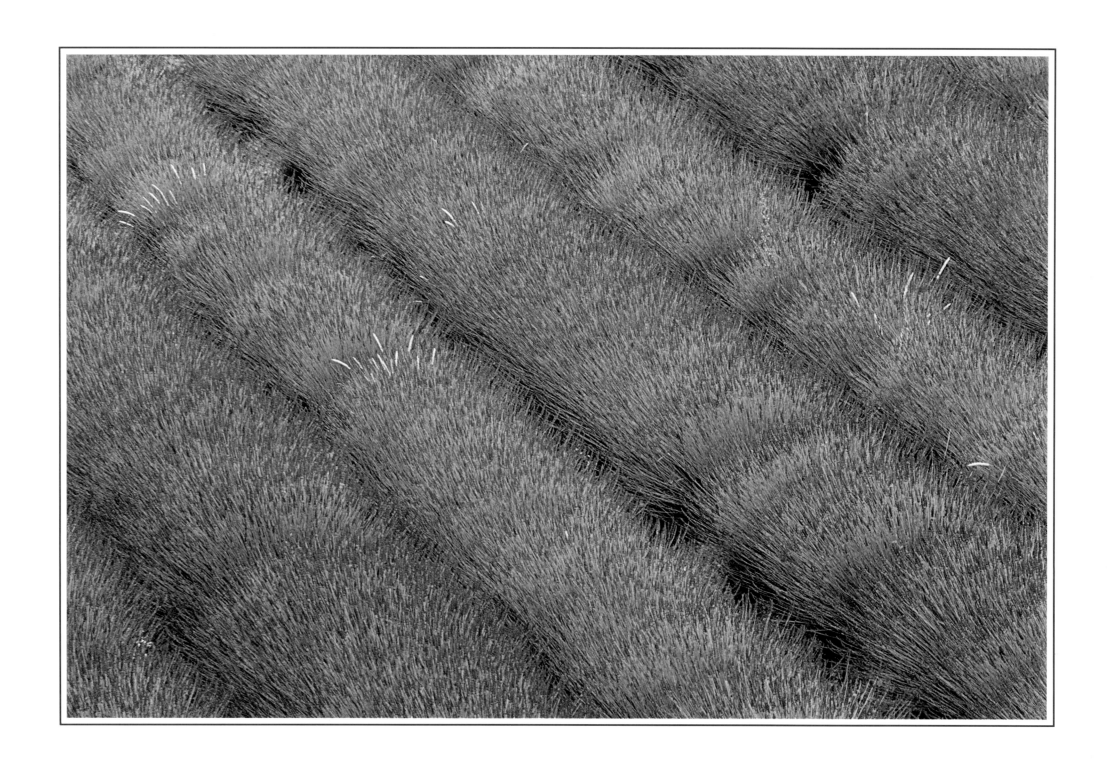

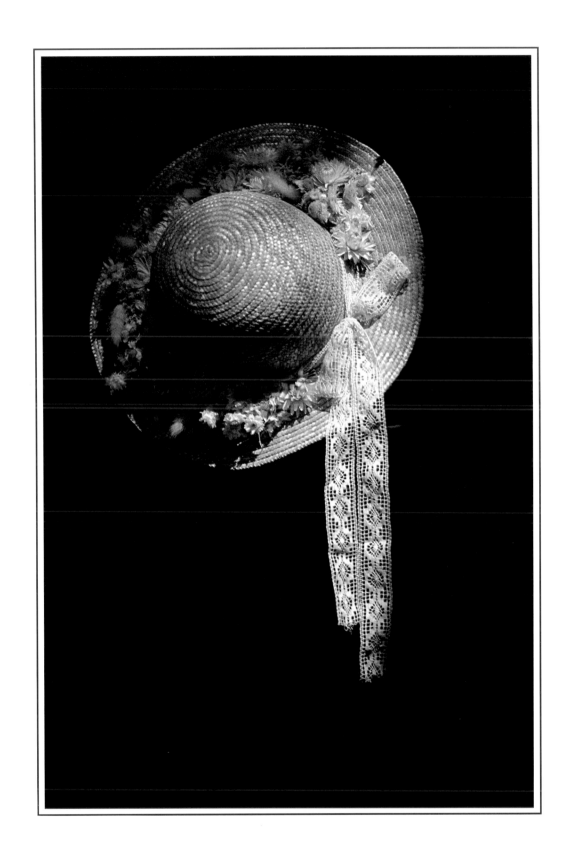

C.ROSSI
tél : 77.40.03

buvez
CHOKY
arôme cacao

arôme
cacao
CHOKY

CATALOGUE

FARMFIELDS BELOW SAULT
OM4 Camera, Zuiko 300 mm,
f8-1/125 sec., tripod.

ROUSSILLON VILLAGE
OM3 Camera, Zuiko Zoom 75-150 mm,
f12-1/250 sec., tripod.

ABANDONED TRACTOR SEAT
OM4 Camera, Zuiko Reflex 500 mm,
f8-1/500 sec.

PLOWING WITH A MULE
OM3 Camera, Zuiko Reflex 500 mm,
f8-1/500 sec.

PRUNING VINEYARDS IN BONNIEUX
OM4 Camera, Zuiko 50 mm,
f9-1/250 sec.

SOWING A FIELD IN THE
LUBERON MOUNTAINS
OM4 Camera, Zuiko Zoom 75-150 mm,
f9-1/250 sec.

CHERRY ORCHARDS AT THE
FOOT OF ROUSSILLON
OM3 Camera, Zuiko Zoom 75-150 mm,
f12-1/60 sec., tripod, polaroid filter.

BLOOMING ALMOND TREE
IN VINEYARD
OM4 Camera, Zuiko Zoom 75-150 mm,
f9-1/250 sec.

ABANDONED FARM AMIDST
SUNFLOWERS AND LAVENDER
OM4 Camera, Zuiko 300 mm,
f9-1/250 sec., tripod.

CHERRY ORCHARDS AND
MUSTARD FIELDS IN BLOOM
OM3 Camera, Zuiko 300 mm,
f6.3-1/500 sec.

MAILTRUCK EN ROUTE THROUGH
LAVENDER AND SUNFLOWER FIELDS
OM4 Camera, Zuiko 300 mm,
f9-1/250 sec., tripod.

CAMARGUE SALT FLATS
WITH SEAGULLS
OM2, Zuiko 300 mm,
f4.5-1/500 sec., polaroid filter.

DRIED SUNFLOWER SEED HEAD
OM4 Camera, Zuiko 500 mm,
f8-1/500 sec., tripod.

FISHERMAN REPAIRING FISH TRAPS
IN THE CAMARGUE
OM2 Camera, 50 mm,
f9-1/250 sec.

SUNFLOWERS IN AVIGNON
OM4 Camera, Zuiko Zoom 75-150 mm,
f9-1/250 sec.

A HORSE RESTS IN THE CAMARGUE,
ITS MANE WINDSWEPT BY THE
"MISTRAL"
OM4 Camera, Zuiko Reflex 500,
f8-1/500 sec.

A MARE WITH HER COLT
IN THE CAMARGUE
OM4 Camera, Zuiko Reflex 500 mm,
f8-1/500 sec.

WINTER LAVENDER
OM3 Camera, Zuiko 300 mm,
f9-1/125 sec., tripod.

LAVENDER BORDERING WHEAT
OM3 Camera, Zuiko Zoom 75-150 mm,
f12-1/125 sec.

VIEW FROM ROUSSILLON
OM3 Camera, 50 mm,
f8-1/125 sec., polaroid filter.

FIELD OF LAVENDER
OM4 Camera, Zuiko Reflex 500 mm,
f8-1/500 sec.

AUTUMN IN THE VINEYARDS
OM4 Camera, Zuiko Zoom 75-150 mm,
f9-1/250 sec.

YOUNG LAVENDER
OM3 Camera, Zuiko 300 mm,
f12-1/125 sec., tripod.

PLANE BRANCHES IN FRONT
OF AN OLD SHUTTER
OM2 Camera, Zuiko Zoom 75-150 mm,
f6.3-1/250 sec.

DECAYING WALL IN ROUSSILLON
OM3 Camera, Zuiko Zoom 75-150 mm,
f8-1/250 sec.

OCHER CANYON IN THE
VICINITY OF ROUSSILLON
OM2 Camera, Zuiko Zoom 75-150 mm,
f16-1/60 sec., tripod.

OCHER CANYON OF ROUSSILLON
OM4 Camera, Zuiko Zoom 75-150 mm,
f11-125 sec.

MOUSTIERS SAINTE MARIE NESTLED
IN THE ALPES DE PROVENCE
OM4 Camera, Zuiko 300 mm,
f9-1/250 sec., tripod.

HOUSE FRONT ON A NARROW STREET
IN ROUSSILLON
OM4 Camera, Zuiko 18 mm,
f5.6-1/60 sec.

LES BAUX DE PROVENCE
OM3 Camera, Zuiko 35 mm,
f11-1/60 sec., polaroid filter.

HOUSE SHUTTER
OM3 Camera, Zuiko 50 mm,
f5.6-1/125 sec.

PLANE ALLEY NEAR
L'ISLE SUR LA SORGUE
OM2 Camera, Zuiko 300 mm,
f12-1/125 sec., tripod.

TREE LINED ENTRANCE TO CHATEAU
DE ROUSSAN NEAR ST. REMY
OM3 Camera, Zuiko 75-150 mm,
f11-1/30 sec., tripod.

HAMLET NEAR APT
OM2 Camera, Zuiko 50 mm,
f12-1/125 sec.

SMALL BARN WITH GORDES VILLAGE
IN BACKGROUND
OM3 Camera, Zuiko Zoom 75-150 mm,
f16-1/125 sec.

WINTER SUNNING IN CADENET
OM4 Camera, Zuiko 50 mm,
f8-1/250 sec.

VIEW THROUGH THE OPENINGS
OF A BARN IN VAISON-LA-ROMAINE
OM3 Camera, Zuiko 35 mm,
f11-1/250 sec.

HOUSE ENTRANCE WITH
DRAPED FLY CURTAIN
OM4 Camera, Zuiko 28 mm,
f9-1/250 sec.

GRAPEVINE SHADOWS ON VILLAGE
HOUSE IN SAULT
OM2 Camera, Zuiko 50 mm,
f9-1/250 sec.

WEATHERED STATUE AT
CHATEAU DE ROUSSAN
OM3 Camera, Zuiko Zoom 75-150 mm,
f12-1/125 sec.

FARM HOUSE IN SIVERGUES
OM4 Camera, Zuiko 75-150 mm,
f11-1/250 sec.

CYCLIST RIDING THROUGH
ROUSSILLON
OM4 Camera, Zuiko Zoom 75-150 mm,
f11-1/250 sec.

CUCURON
OM2 Camera, Zuiko 50 mm,
f11-1/250 sec.

WINTER STREET LIFE
OM2 Camera, Zuiko 50 mm,
f8-1/250 sec.

ST. SATURNIN D'APT
OM2 Camera, Zuiko Zoom 75-150 mm,
f8-1/250 sec.

ON THE PLAINS NEAR ST. PANTALEON
OM2 Camera, Zuiko Zoom 75-150 mm,
f12-1/60 sec., polaroid filter.

ROWS OF MINIATURE PLASTIC
«HOT HOUSES»
SHELTERED FROM THE WIND BY CANE
OM4 Camera, Zuiko 50 mm,
f8-1/125 sec.

SNOW COVERED CHERRY ORCHARDS
IN MURS
OM2 Camera, Zuiko 300 mm,
f11-1/250 sec., tripod.

SNOW DUSTING ON THE VINEYARDS
OF THE LUBERON MOUNTAINS
OM2 Camera, Zuiko 35 mm,
f11-1/250 sec.

FARMER'S FIRES OF BRUSH
IN THE EARLY MORNING
OM2 Camera, Zuiko Zoom 75-150 mm,
f6.3-1/125

PRUNED TREE AND AN OLD
FARM HOUSE
OM2 Camera, Zuiko 50 mm,
f11-1/250 sec.

HILLSIDE VILLAGE OF ROUSSILLON
OM2 Camera, Zuiko 50 mm,
f9-1/250 sec.

STORM CLOUDS AND SUNSET COLLIDE
IN TREE ALLEYS OF THE PLAINS
BELOW GORDES
OM2 Camera, Zuiko 18 mm,
f6.3-1/125 sec.

ROADSIDE SHRINE NEAR MURS
OM3 Camera, Zuiko 75-150 mm,
f9-1/250

MORNING FOG LIFTS IN THE
VICINITY OF GOULT
OM2 Camera, Zuiko 300 mm,
f11-1/125 sec., tripod.

ARCHES OF THE ARLES
ARENA JUXTAPOSED
WITH THE STEEPLES AND
TOWERS OF THE MEDIEVAL TIMES
OM4 Camera, Zuiko Zoom 75-150 mm,
f16-1/60 sec., tripod and polaroid filter

TOWN PLAZA OF ROBION
OM4 Camera, Zuiko Zoom 28-48 mm,
f9-1/250 sec.

WINE COOPERATIVE OF ROGNES
OM2 Camera, Zuiko 50 mm,
f9-1/250 sec.

TOWN CRIER OF L'ISLE SUR LA SORGUE
OM2 Camera, Zuiko 35 mm,
f6.3 - 1/60 sec.

MAN OF PROVENCE
OM3 Camera, Zuiko Reflex 500 mm,
f8-1/500 sec.

THOR STREET SCENE
OM4 Camera, Zuiko 50 mm,
f9-1/125 sec.

PEASANT ON THE WAY TO
BOULES GAME
OM2 Camera, Zuiko Zoom 75-150 mm,
f5.6-1/250

COVERALLS DECORATE A WASHLINE
IN APT
OM2 Camera, Zuiko Zoom 75-150 mm,
f8-1/125 sec.

LAUNDRY DISPLAY IN SAULT
OM2 Camera, Zuiko 50 mm,
f8-1/250 sec.

COSTUMED CELEBRATION
IN ROUSILLON
OM4 Camera, Zuiko Zoom 28-48 mm,
f8-1/250 sec.

WEDDING VEHICLES AT CITY HALL
IN ARLES
OM4 Camera, Zuiko Zoom 28-48 mm,
f9-1/250 sec.

A LADY OF ARLES AT THE
FESTIVAL OF THE QUEEN
OM3 Camera, Zuiko 300 mm,
f4.5-1/500 sec.

DRIED FLOWER DISPLAY AT MARKET
IN ARLES
OM4 Camera, Zuiko Zoom 75-150 mm,
f8-1/250 sec.

STRAW HAT WITH DRIED FLOWERS
AND LACE
OM4 Camera, Zuiko Zoom 75-150 mm,
f5.6-1/250 sec.

FLOWER VENDOR WITH CHURCH
REFLECTION AT SUNDAY MARKET
IN L'ISLE SUR LA SORGUE
OM2 Camera, 50 mm,
f9-1/60 sec.

CAFE TERRACE IN ARLES
OM4 Camera, Zuiko 50 mm,
f6.3-1/250 sec.

VEGETABLE VENDOR IN APT
OM2 Camera, 50 mm,
f6.3-1/125 sec.

NECTARINES AND MELONS AT
THE ARLES MARKET
OM3 Camera, Zuiko Zoom 28-48 mm,
f9-1/250 sec.

POULTRY VENDOR CLOSING DOWN
OM2 Camera, Zuiko Zoom 75-150 mm,
f8-1/250 sec.

PLASTIC NURSERY GREENHOUSE
OM2 Camera, Zuiko Zoom 75-150 mm,
f8-1/125 sec.

TERRACE CAFE IN ARLES
OM4 Camera, Zuiko Zoom 28-48 mm
f9-1/250 sec.

VILLAGE CAFE IN THE LUBERON
OM4 Camera, Zuiko Zoom 75-150 mm,
f9-1/250 sec.

STATUE OF FREDERIC MISTRAL
IN PLACE DU FORUM, ARLES
OM4 Camera, Zuiko Zoom 75-150 mm
f12-1/125 sec., tripod.

TWILIGHT ON THE HILLSIDE VILLAGE
OF GORDES
OM4 Camera, Zuiko 50 mm,
f5.6-1/30 sec., tripod.

As in past books of mine, I hope that this book is viewed as if it were an exhibition with very little concern by the viewer for titles, place or time. My tendency when photographing is to free myself of labels and prejudices that would hinder me from pure discovery in form and color, be it in a rural or an urban setting.

While searching for sympathetic situations to photograph these many years, I have had to consider equipping myself with cameras and lenses that satisfy a variety of needs. When discovering a detail or a distant image, a broad system of sharp lenses and light cameras was essential to ease the burden of weight when traveling. For nearly fifteen years now the Olympus cameras and Zuiko lenses have served me well. Through these years as I exchanged OM1 for OM2 and presently for the fine standards of OM3 and OM4, satisfaction has remained intact.

My film is always Kodachrome 64 for its fine grain, fidelity to colors, and reasonable speed (ASA).
With usually two cameras hanging from my neck, I walk through the fields and villages, seeking the right perspective. My senses are fine-tuned, and the technical support systems are ready to facilitate my observations. Via the camera, I enjoy life a great deal.

Dennis Stock

ANTHOLEGIES
Let us begin, Ridge Press, 1961.
Creative America, Ridge Press, 1962.
America in crisis, Holt, Rinehart and Winston, 1969.
Photography in the Twentieth Century, Horizon Press, 1967.
Photography in America, Random House, 1974.
Paris/Magnum, Aperture, 1981.
James Dean, St. Martin's Press, 1984.

DOCUMENTARY FILMS
«Efforts to Provoke» / United Artists.
«Quest» / Cinema Center / CBS.
«British Youth» / NBC

Major magazine contributions include:
LIFE, LOOK, HOLIDAY, VENTURE, REALITIES, PARIS
MATCH, QUEEN, GEO, STERN and BUNTE.

Articles on Dennis Stock have appeared in:
ASAHI CAMERA (1956), CAMERA (1962, 1967, 1976), MO-
DERN PHOTOGRAPHY (1966), INFINITY (1967), APPLIED
PHOTOGRAPHY (1968), ZOOM (1972), NUOVA FOTOGRA-
FIA (1973), POPULAR PHOTOGRAPHY (1978), DOUBLE-
PAGE (1981, 1982), I GRANDI FOTOGRAFI / Fabbri (1982),
NEW YORK TIMES MAGAZINE (1984) and BRITISH PHO-
TOGRAPHY (1987).

He has also been the subject of a NATIONAL EDUCATION-
AL TELEVISION PROFILE (1958), and has been featured in
a program produced by NATIONAL ITALIAN TELEVISION
- RAI (1971).

MAJOR COLLECTIONS
Art Institute of Chicago.
Kunsthaus, Zurich.
International Center of Photography, New York.
Creative Center for Photography, University of Arizona.
George Eastman House, Rochester.
Musee d'Art Moderne, Paris.
Fotografiska Museet, Stockholm, Sweden.

AWARDS
First Prize, Life Young Photographers, 1951.
First Prize, International Photography, Poland, 1962.

ONE-MAN PHOTOGRAPHY EXHIBITIONS
Chicago Art Institute, 1963 (purchased for permanent collec-
tion).
Form Gallery, Zurich, 1966.
DeYoung Museum, San Francisco, 1970.
Traveling color exhibition on the theme of "The Sun", origi-
nating at Eastman House, Rochester, 1967-1974.
Woodstock Artist's Association, Woodstock, NewYork, 1973.
Sony Gallery, Tokyo, 1974.
Alpha Cubic Gallery, Tokyo, 1976.
Retrospective exhibition at the International Center of Photog-
raphy, New York, 1977.
Photofind Gallery, Woodstock, New York, 1985.
Urban Gallery, New York, 1987.

GROUP EXHIBITIONS
"Photography at Mid-Century," George Eastman House, 1959.
"The World as Seen by Magnum Photographers," traveling
exhibition, 1960.
"Man's Humanity to Man," Red Cross Centenial, Geneva, 1962.
"Photography in the Twentieth Century," traveling exhibition
prepared by the George Eastman House for the National Gal-
lery of Canada, 1967.
"Photography in America," Whitney Museum of American
Art, New York, 1974.
Arles Photography Festival, Arles France, 1976 and 1977.
"Magnum Paris," Luxembourg Museum, Paris, 1982.
"Jazz et Photographie," Musee d'Art Moderne, Paris, 1983.

WORKSHOPS AND LECTURE
New York University.
International Center of Photography, New York.
New School for Social Research, New York.
Pratt Institute, New York.
State University of New York, Stony Brook.
Festival d'Arles, France.
Center for Photography, Woodstock, New York.

BIOGRAPHICAL
Born in New York City, 1928.
Apprenticed to Gjon Mili, 1947-1951.
Member of «Magnum Photos» since 1951.
Currently resides in Woodstock, New York.

AUTHORED PHOTOGRAPHY BOOKS
Portrait of a young man, James Dean, Kadokava Shoten, 1956.
Plaisir du Jazz, La Guilde du Livre, 1959.
Jazz Welt, Hatje, 1959.
Jazz Street, Doubleday, 1960.
California Trip, Grossman, 1970.
The Alternative, Macmillan, 1970.
Living our Future: Francis of Assisi, Franciscan Herald, 1972.
Edge of Life: World of the Estuary, Sierra Club Books, 1972.
National Parks Centenial Portfolio, Sierra Club Books, 1972.
Brother Sun, Sierra Club Books, 1974.
California the Golden Coast, Viking Press, 1974.
The Circle of Seasons, Viking Press, 1974.
A Haiku Journey, Kodansha International, 1974.
This Land of Europe, Kodansha International, 1976.
Voyage poetique a tavers le Japon d'autre fois, Bibliotheque
des Arts, 1976.
Alaska, Harry Abrams Publishing, 1978.
James Dean revisited, Viking/Penguin, 1978.
America Seen, Contrejour, 1980.
St. Francis in Assisi, Scala/Harper and Row, 1981.
Flower Show, Rizzoli/Magnus, 1986.
James Dean revisited, Shirmer & Mosel, 1986, Chronicle Books,
1987.
Provence Memories, NewYork Graphic Society/Magnus, 1988.
Hawaii, Harry Abrams Publishing, 1988.

Printed and bound in Italy by Grafiche Lema - Maniago/Pordenone